This Book Presented To:

dear Ann & Jim.... I see how amazing God made you and your precious families. How special it will be to share again. God's blessings always.

Given With Great JOY! From:

Blessing & love, Kathy

A Note to Parents, Grandparents and Caregivers

You have been given a precious gift from God, *A CHILD TO LOVE!* With this gift comes the wonderful responsibility to provide physical care, affection, encouragement, correction, protection and love to every child entrusted to us.

"I See How Amazing God Made Me" is designed to guide and encourage children to care for their bodies. The whimsical illustrations and delightful words will capture a child's imagination and ignite their desire to live a healthy and happy life that God intended for them.

The mission of this book is to produce healthy choices through the positive, repetitive framework of the **"I See, I Can, I Will"** concept.

- "I See" sparks the imagination within a child
- "I Can" ignites the willpower within a child
- "I Will" blazes the path for success within a child

May this book inspire, motivate and empower you and your child.

I See How Amazing GOD Made Me

Simple words and delightful artwork to bring out the best in our children while they care for their bodies.

Written by
Kathy Nelson

Illustrated by
Kim Sponaugle

Text copyright © 2012 by Kathleen (Kathy) Nelson. All rights reserved
Illustrations by Kim Sponaugle. All rights reserved

I See How Amazing God Made Me
ISBN 978-0-9854648-0-6

1st printing, April 2012

No part of this book may be reproduced or transmitted
in any form or by any means without written permission
from the author, Kathy Nelson.

Scripture quotation are taken from the Holy Bible,
New International Version – 10th Anniversary Edition, Copyright © 1995

Formatted by Clark Kidman, Design Type Service, Salt Lake City, UT
Printed in the U.S.A. by Artistic Printing, Salt Lake City, UT

A Ministry Department of Artists in Christian Testimony Intl
www.ACTinternational.org

Ministry of "I See, I Can, I Will Support a Child In Need", P.O. Box 564
Midway, UT 84049 – 720-219-6399 – Isee.Ican.Iwill@gmail.com
Website: http://www.iseeicaniwill.com

*This book is dedicated to precious
Mason, Roman and London*

*May you always seek our sweet Jesus,
His wise wisdom, His powerful peace and
His perfect love!*

I See How Amazing God Made Me

When I look in the mirror, I see how amazing God made me.
He gave me curious ears to hear and charming eyes to see.

He gave me strong arms for fun,
and fast legs to run.

He gave me toes and fingers, all that can wiggle.
And a beautiful mouth to smile and giggle.

I see, I can, I will
take good care of the body
that God made for me.

I See

bubbles floating way up high.
Could there be a bubble filled with love floating by?

I Can

soak and splash as I scrub and rub.
Dipping and twirling is so cool in the tub.

I can wash my body clean and neat.
Just look, I have no dirty hands or feet.

Another bubble is dancing by.
Is it singing me a sweet song and saying good-bye?

I Will

take good care of the body
that God has made for me.

I See

lots of bubbly suds as I shampoo my hair,
sparkling soapsuds falling everywhere.

I Can

gently comb the tangles from my long soft hair.
It's so fun to add shampoo and do it with care.

With a swirl of the suds going all around,
I look like a funny circus clown.

But wait! I can rinse all the suds away,
so I'll look like an angel today.

I Will

take good care of the hair
that God has made for me.

I See

brushing my teeth is a special treat.
My toothbrush makes my smile look so sweet.

I Can

brush my teeth every morning and every night.
It makes them look shiny and bright.

Up and down and all-around, this is how it goes.
I love brushing my teeth while standing on my toes.

Brushing and flossing is what I should do.
I can swish, swash and spit the water out too.

I Will

take good care of the teeth
that God has made for me.

I See

fun toys that say "Get up, let's go play."
I say "Friends, let's hurry and not delay."

I Can

bend and stretch my body in most every way.
I can hop and dance and jump and say.

"Come outside and join me, it's a beautiful day!
Our bodies become strong as we exercise every day."

Playing with good friends is the best.
We run and laugh until our bodies need rest.

I Will

take good care of the body and mind
that God has made for me.

I See

healthy food that looks so yummy.

Surely it will stop the rumbling in my tummy.

I Can

eat breakfast, lunch and dinner.

Eating three meals a day makes me a winner.

I can eat my fruits and veggies, too.

Fueling up with nature's best is what I like to do.

Drinking lots of water is the way to go.

I remind myself to drink it slow.

I Will

choose to eat healthy to take good care of my body

that God has made for me.

I See

God's beautiful rainbow shining so bright.
My friends and I shout out with delight.

"It is true, there is no one in the world
that is exactly like me or you."

I Can

care for my body and give God all the glory.
Jesus loves me! I'm part of his wondrous story.
Through prayer I can talk with God each and every day,
and tell Him, "Thank You Jesus for loving me and making me this way!"

I Will

take good care of my body
that God has made for me.

"I PRAISE YOU BECAUSE I AM FEARFULLY AND WONDERFULLY MADE; YOUR WORKS ARE WONDERFUL" Psalm 139:14

A special thank you for your love and support.

**Your love has
given me great joy and encouragement.
Philemon 1:7**

For those who have brought life to the "I See, I Can, I Will" concept. Thank you!

- To the glory of God, thank you Jesus for bringing forth your ideas
- To my devoted husband, Wayne, for being my best friend and supporter
- To my precious daughter, Jennifer, and dear son-in-law, Dave, for their encouragement, inspiration and belief in the ministry of "I See, I Can, I Will Support a Child In Need"
- To my blessed grandchildren, Mason, Roman and London who keep me young and laughing
- To my beloved Mother and dear family for their encouragement and love
- To my dear friends . . . Pastor Cliff and Linda, Pastor Steve and Jackie, Lois and Keith, Carol and Steve, Dr. Ron and Hillary, Connie and Kevin, Demetria and Richard, Joan and Steve for their prayers, their solid advice and their amazing support
- To a gifted artist, Kim Sponaugle, for her adorable illustrations

I appreciate you all!

Blessings in Jesus Christ,
Kathy

About the Author

Kathy Nelson is an author who believes a story shared between a child and an adult is a precious moment always to be cherished. Her consistent theme of "I See, I Can, I Will" are delightful simple words to encourage a child in making positive choices. The lively rhymes portray lessons of love and encouragement for children of all ages. Sharing God's word and His amazing love is a true passion for Kathy. Kathy and her husband Wayne live in Midway, Utah.

Please visit Kathy at http://www.iseeicaniwill.com.

About the Illustrator

Kim Sponaugle's is an award-winning illustrator who portrays the charm of children. Kim is a wife and mom, living in southern New Jersey. She has illustrated more than 36 books for kids. Kim is amazed how God has given her a vocation that is so enjoyable. Soli Deo Gloria!

Please visit Kim at www.picturekitchenstudio.com